NORRIE EXPLORES...

CAPE TOWN

Help Norrie to solve the clues on a fascinating adventure!

World Book, Inc.
180 North LaSalle Street
Suite 900
Chicago, Illinois 60601
USA

For information about other World Book publications, visit our website at www.worldbook.com or call 1-800-WORLDBK (967-5325). For information about sales to schools and libraries, call 1-800-975-3250 (United States), or 1-800-837-5365 (Canada).

Library of Congress Cataloging-in-Publication Data for this volume has been applied for.

Norrie Explores ...
ISBN: 978-0-7166-5303-5 (set, hc.)

Norrie Explores ... Cape Town
ISBN: 978-0-7166-5306-6 (hc.)
ISBN: 978-0-7166-5326-4 (pf.)

Also available as:
ISBN: 978-0-7166-5316-5 (e-book)

Staff

Executive Committee
President: Geoff Broderick
Vice President, Editorial: Tom Evans
Vice President, Finance: Donald D. Keller
Vice President, International: Eddy Kisman
Vice President, Technology: Jason Dole
Director, Human Resources: Bev Ecker

Editorial
Senior Editor/Indexer: Shawn Brennan
Editor/Researcher: Lynn Durbin
Content Creator: Jenna Neely
Curriculum Designer: Caroline Davidson
Project Coordinator: Kaile Kilner
Proofreader: Nathalie Strassheim

Graphics and Design
Senior Visual Communications Designer: Melanie Bender
Senior Media Editor: Rosalia Bledsoe

Acknowledgments

Writer: Izzi Howell
Illustrator: Jon Davis

Developed with World Book by
White-Thomson Publishing LTD
www.wtpub.co.uk

Cover: Norrie artwork by Jon Davis, Advocate Art; © Sebastien Lecocq, Alamy Images

4-5 © wolffpower/Shutterstock
6-7 © Ian Dagnall, Alamy; © Marcel Alsemgeest, Shutterstock
8-9 © Shutterstock
10-11 © mauritius images GmbH/Alamy Images; © Schnepf Design, Shutterstock; © Efimova Anna, Shutterstock
12-13 © Valeri Potapova, Shutterstock; © Jeffrey Isaac Greenberg 19+/Alamy Images
14-15 ©meunierd/Shutterstock; © Design Pics Inc/Alamy Images
16-17 © Lucian Coman, Shutterstock; © Ulrich Doering, Alamy Images
18-19 © Shutterstock
20-21 © Ilyas Ayub, Alamy Images; © Andrea Willmore, Shutterstock
22-23 © EQRoy/Shutterstock; © Mattes René, SuperStock
24-25 © Antony Souter, Alamy Images; © Dimple Patel, Alamy Images; © BlueOrange Studio/Shutterstock
26-27 © David South, Alamy Images; © M.Sobreira, Alamy Images
28-29 © Kyoko Uchida, Alamy Images; © Gallo Images, Alamy Images
30-31 © Jeffrey Isaac Greenberg 19+/Alamy Images; © EcoPrint/Shutterstock
32-33 © Shutterstock
34-35 © Henrique NDR Martins, iStock; © TUX85/Shutterstock; © SL-Photography/Shutterstock
36-37 © Sebastien Lecocq, Alamy Images; © Cathy Withers-Clarke, Shutterstock
38-39 © Hemis/Alamy Images; © Jono0001/iStock; © Maurizio De Mattei, Shutterstock
40-41 © Handmade Pictures/Shutterstock; © Burhan Ay, Alamy Images
42-43 © Shutterstock
46-47 © Aninka Bongers-Sutherland, Shutterstock; © Juergen Wallstabe, Shutterstock; © Paul Gregg, Travel Africa/Alamy Images; © Jeffrey Isaac Greenberg 16+/Alamy Images; © Moobatto/Shutterstock; © Punctu8/Dreamstime
48-49 © Eric Nathan, Alamy Images; © Stories from Anywhere/Shutterstock; © Rodger Shagam, africanpix/Alamy Images; © Mike Hutchings, Reuters/Alamy Images; © John Martin Media, Shutterstock; © Jeffrey Isaac Greenberg 3+/Alamy Images
50-51 © Shutterstock

Contents

Welcome to Cape Town!

Hi, I'm Norrie! I'm a puffin. I love to travel the world and explore different cities around the globe.

Today, I'm in Cape Town, one of the largest cities in South Africa. South Africa is a country on the continent of Africa. Have you ever visited Cape Town or South Africa before?

Most countries have only one capital. South Africa has three: Cape Town, Pretoria, and Bloemfontein. Each one is home to a different branch of government. Cape Town is the legislative capital – the place where people meet to make and change laws.

Cape Town looks like an amazing city! I can't wait to explore it!

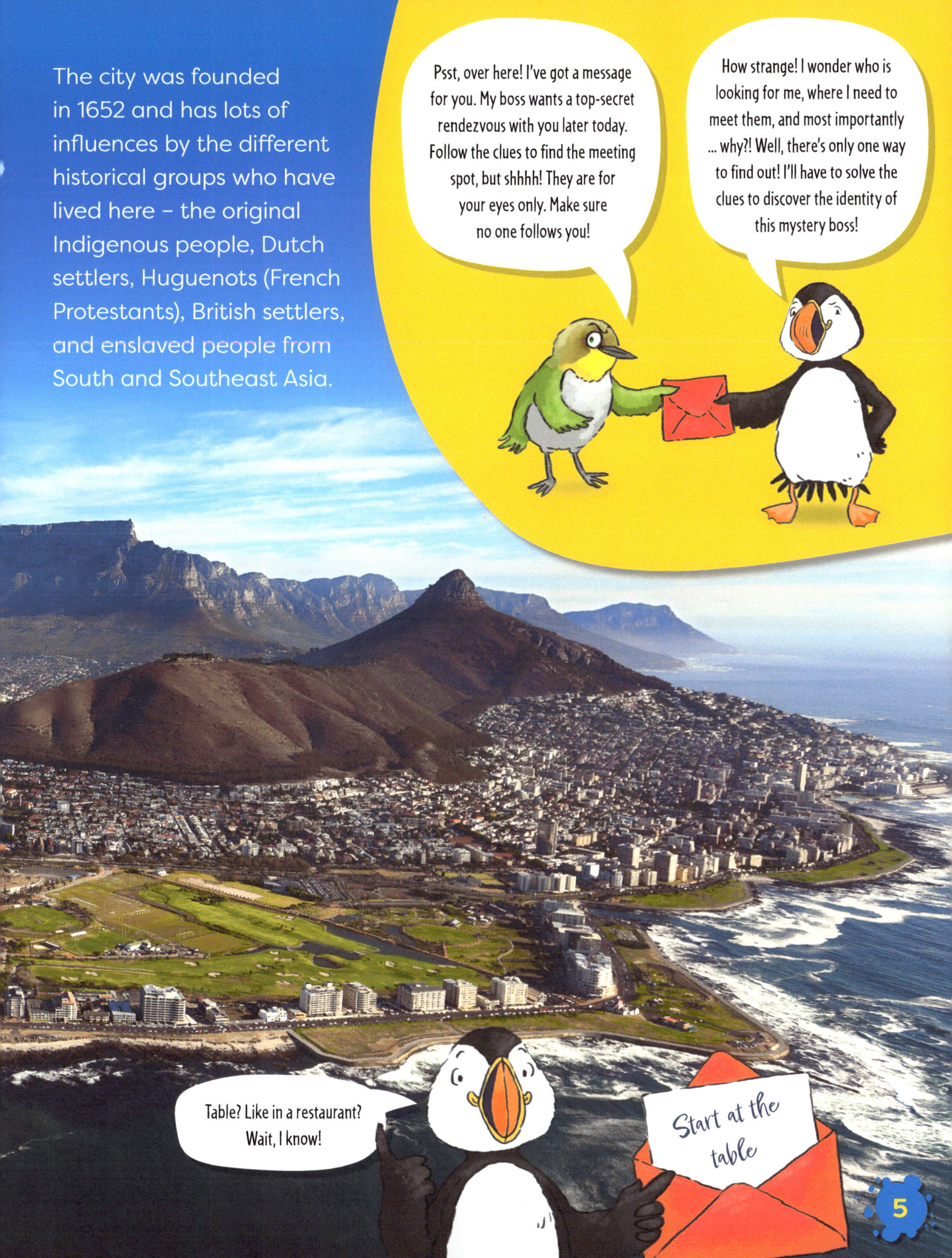
The city was founded in 1652 and has lots of influences by the different historical groups who have lived here – the original Indigenous people, Dutch settlers, Huguenots (French Protestants), British settlers, and enslaved people from South and Southeast Asia.
Psst, over here! I've got a message for you. My boss wants a top-secret rendezvous with you later today. Follow the clues to find the meeting spot, but shhhh! They are for your eyes only. Make sure no one follows you!
How strange! I wonder who is looking for me, where I need to meet them, and most importantly ... why?! Well, there's only one way to find out! I'll have to solve the clues to discover the identity of this mystery boss!
Table? Like in a restaurant? Wait, I know!
Start at the table

Table Mountain

The most famous table in Cape Town *has* to be Table Mountain. The top of the mountain is flat – just like a table!

You can hike up to the top or take the cable car. It's like a little car that is pulled along thick wires called cables. It's 900 feet (3,000 meters) to the top of Table Mountain, so I think I'll take the cable car today!

You can see all of Cape Town from the top of Table Mountain. See how the city is squeezed between the mountains and Table Bay? Cape Town has grown a lot. To the north, the ocean stretches beyond the city and Table Bay. To the south, there are mountains on the Cape Peninsula.

This cute little animal is a rock hyrax but everyone here calls it a dassie. It looks like a big hamster, doesn't it? But its closest living relative is actually the African elephant!

A peninsula is an area of land almost surrounded by water. On one side of this peninsula is the Atlantic Ocean. On the other side is False Bay. You might hear another name for the peninsula while you're here: the Cape of Good Hope. The city gets its name from this cape. A cape is a piece of land that sticks out into the ocean.

Hmmm, these clues are difficult!

From mountain to bay

Table Bay

Beneath Table Mountain and just beyond the downtown shoreline lies Table Bay. It was named after Table Mountain.

In 1652, a Dutch ship captain named Jan van Riebeeck sailed into Table Bay. He worked for a big business called the Dutch East India Company. The company brought spices and silk to Europe from the islands of Southeast Asia, once known as the East Indies. Table Bay was around the halfway point for ships making the journey.

Riebeeck came to set up a refreshment station – a place where sailors could stop to get fresh food and water, fix their boats, and rest. Van Riebeeck's job was to build a fort, plant a vegetable garden, and trade cattle with the Indigenous people who lived here. His refreshment station was the beginning of European settlement in South Africa.

Today, the Cape Town port in Table Bay is the second largest port in South Africa. Many ships stop off to refuel and pick up supplies. Cruise ships also dock here, picking up and dropping off tourists.

Victoria & Alfred Waterfront

Do you see the big red clock tower? It's here at the Victoria & Alfred Waterfront.

Look at all the stores, restaurants, and people! It was crowded in the late 1800's, too. That's when many people arrived on ships to work in the area's gold and diamond mines. We can find out more about diamond mining at the Cape Town Diamond Museum.

There are plenty of other attractions here too, including a giant Ferris wheel, an aquarium, boat trips, and a modern art museum. The waterfront is also a working harbor, so you may see a ship being repaired or picking up fresh supplies.

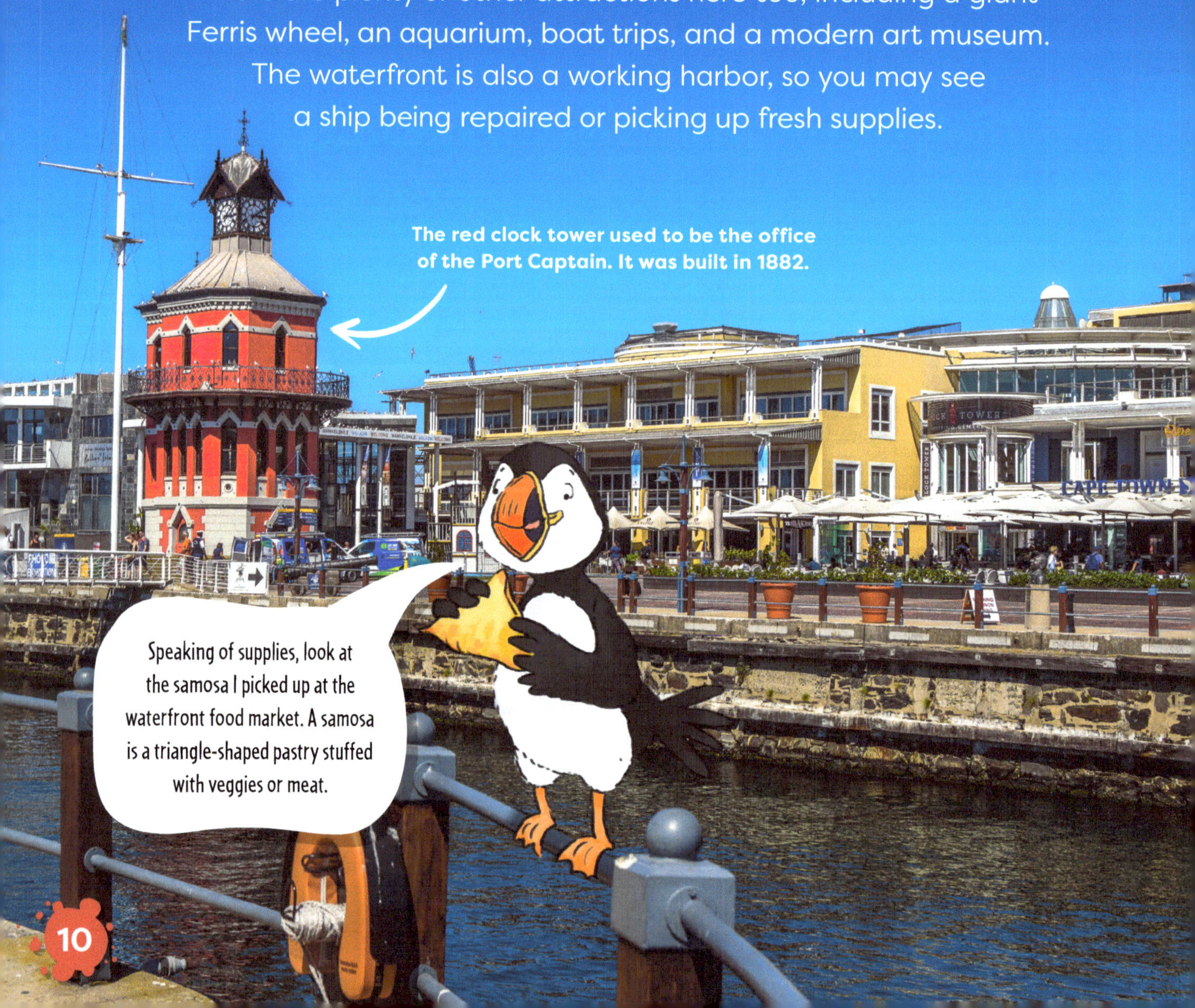

The red clock tower used to be the office of the Port Captain. It was built in 1882.

Speaking of supplies, look at the samosa I picked up at the waterfront food market. A samosa is a triangle-shaped pastry stuffed with veggies or meat.

The waterfront is named after Queen Victoria of Great Britain, who lived from 1819 to 1901, and her second son. Alfred lived from 1844 to 1900. Dutch people founded Cape Town in 1652. The British occupied the area starting in 1795.

Two Oceans Aquarium

I've had a good look at the sea around Cape Town from above, but what kind of wildlife is hiding under the waves?

You can take a look without getting wet at the Two Oceans Aquarium on the Victoria & Alfred Waterfront. The aquarium is named after the two oceans that meet off the coast of Cape Town – the Atlantic Ocean and the Indian Ocean. It is home to animals from both oceans, as well as certain species that are only found off the coast of South Africa, such as the Knysna seahorse.

This tank of western clownfish has a special glass dome so you can experience life underwater for yourself.

Whoa, it's like I'm swimming with the clownfish!

There are many incredible exhibits at the Two Oceans Aquarium, including a massive kelp forest and a special shark tank. About 100 kinds of shark live in ocean waters off the coast of South Africa. You can get up close and personal with some of these species at the aquarium, without the risk of getting bitten!

Robben Island

Today, Robben Island is a museum, but it used to be a prison.

The most famous prisoner here was Nelson Mandela. He spent 18 of his 27 years in prison on Robben Island. Why was he in jail? Mandela worked against a way of government called apartheid. Apartheid is an Afrikaans word that means separateness. Under apartheid, laws kept white and nonwhite people separated. Apartheid laws were unfair and harmful to nonwhite people.

In the museum, you can take a tour of the prison buildings and visit the quarries (rock mines) where the prisoners worked.

Nelson Mandela was let out of prison in 1990. A year later, the last apartheid laws were repealed (canceled). People of any color could go to the same schools and live in the same neighborhoods. In 1994, nonwhite people were allowed to vote for the first time. Nelson Mandela was elected president of South Africa.

This was Nelson Mandela's cell. It was very small and basic.

The island is also a nature reserve. If you're lucky, you might spot such animals as tortoises, a type of antelope called the springbok, and fur seals. The name *Robben* is actually a Dutch word meaning seals. So Robben Island actually means "Seal Island"! I think I might be the only puffin, though.

Football? In Cape Town? I know just the place!

Cape Town Stadium

Cape Town Stadium was built for the 2010 World Cup football tournament, and is still used for many football matches today.

Football here is the game people in Canada and the United States call soccer. South Africa is a nation that loves sports. In Cape Town, football brings out the biggest crowds. Games called rugby and cricket are also popular. These used to be whites-only sports in South Africa. But that changed after apartheid ended in 1991.

As well as football games, Cape Town Stadium also hosts rugby and tennis matches, and concerts. It has over 55,000 seats, so many people can come to enjoy these events. South African sports fans love to sing their country's national anthem at international sports matches.

The anthem combines songs of black Africans and white settlers. When you sing it, you speak five different languages! There are sections of the song in Xhosa, Zulu, Sesotho, Afrikaans, and English. What is your country's national anthem?

In South Africa, football fans cheer with colorful plastic horns called vuvuzelas. It can get very noisy during matches! Have you ever heard a vuvuzela before?

Castle of Good Hope

This large, yellow building is the Castle of Good Hope. Hmmm ... a yellow castle. I must be in the right place!

This is the oldest colonial building in South Africa. Dutch colonists and the people they enslaved built the Castle of Good Hope to defend their outpost against British invaders. It was finished in 1679. The castle held more than just soldiers. It was like a small town inside. There were apartments, a church, a bakery, offices, and even jail cells.

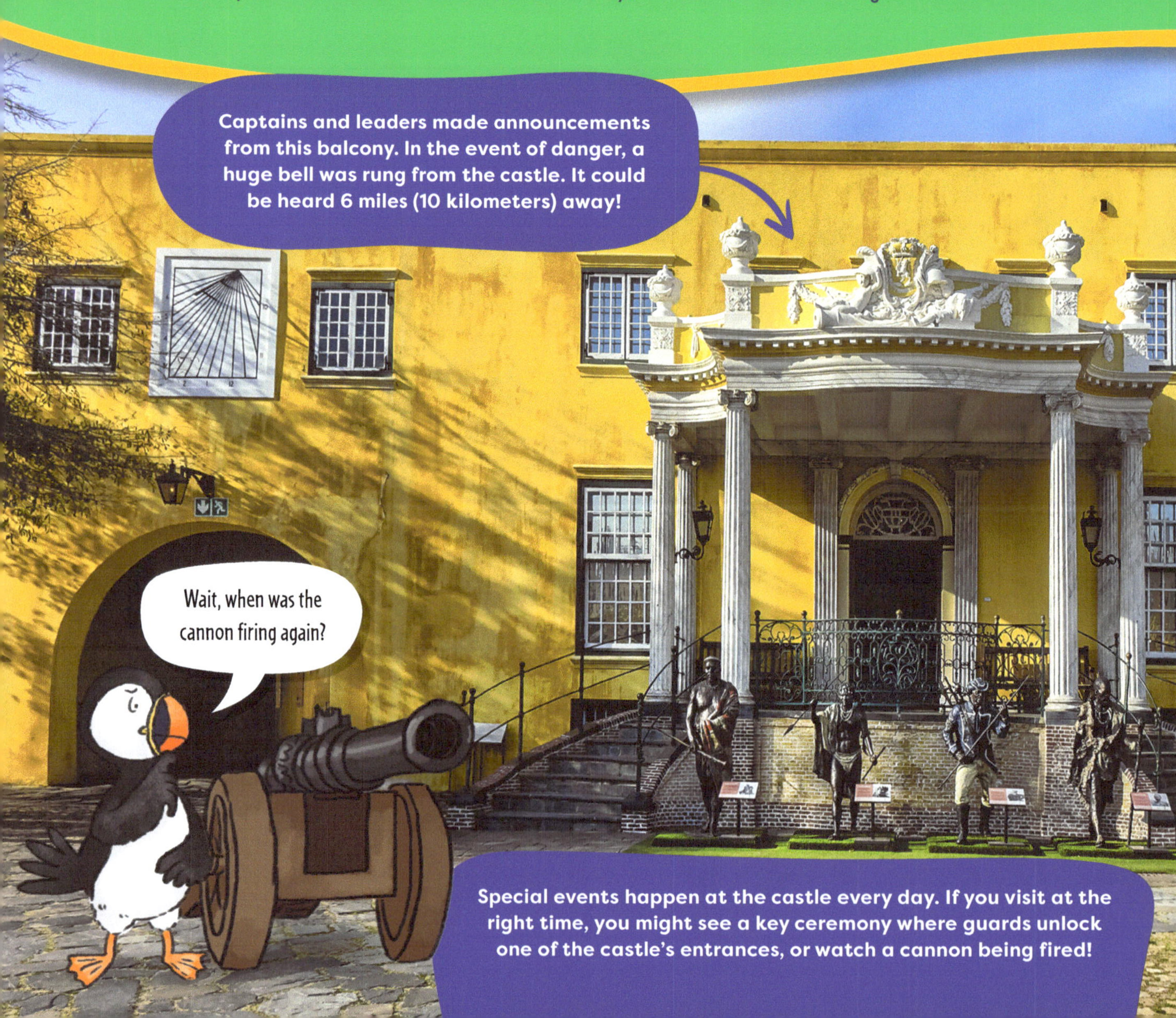

Do you notice anything unusual about the castle's shape? It was built in the shape of a five-pointed star! The points of the star are known as bastions. The shape of the castle meant that soldiers could defend it from an attack from any direction.

The Castle of Good Hope became a national monument in 1936. Today, you can look around the castle and explore its walls and moat. There are also several museums, including a military museum and an art museum. So there's something for everyone!

The Company's Garden

The Company's Garden is the perfect place to rest and relax.

I'm feeling a bit tired after a busy morning of sightseeing, so I'm glad my trail of clues has led me here. The Company's Garden is located right near the Castle of Good Hope. It is actually the oldest garden in South Africa. It was planted in the 1650's. Vegetables were grown here for sailors on the Dutch East India Company's trading ships. They grew such vegetables as peas, beans, spinach, cabbage, and much more. In 1898, the gardens were made public. Capetonians and visitors have enjoyed coming here ever since!

This statue commemorates all the South African soldiers who died fighting in World War I (1914-1918).

Here you go!

The Company's Garden is famous for its friendly squirrels. You can even buy special bags of squirrel food for them here!

Today, the main gardens aren't used for growing vegetables, but they are home to many large trees and plants, an herb garden, and a rose garden. There are walkways lined with trees, historical statues, and ponds filled with fish. In 2014, a small vegetable garden was planted, inspired by the original vegetable gardens from the 1650's. The vegetables grown here are used by a restaurant in the Company's Garden.

District Six Museum

District Six was a neighborhood that used to stand on this exact spot. But it doesn't exist any more.

Here's what happened. Long ago, people of different colors lived side by side in District Six. The neighborhood was alive with many types of food, music, and culture. But in 1966, during apartheid, a new law said only white people could live in District Six. More than 60,000 nonwhite people were forced to move. Bulldozers flattened their homes. Families and friends who had lived in District Six for many years were sent to separate, sometimes faraway neighborhoods, called townships. Their tiny new homes were made of scrap metal sheets.

You can take a guided tour of the museum. The guides have many stories to tell about living with no electric power, running water, or bathrooms. You can also see reconstructions of destroyed rooms. That means the rooms have been rebuilt to show what they used to look like.

During apartheid, nonwhite people were separated from white people in many ways, from which benches they could sit on to which schools and hospitals they could go to.

There is a map of District Six on the floor so you can see the different roads.
COWLEY STREET
RUTGER STREET
RUTGER STREET
PONTAC STREET
CHAPEL STREET
BLOEMHOF
RUSSELL STREET
ASPELING STREET
ST PHILLIP STREET
STUCKERIS STREET
UPPER ASHLEY STREET
MOUNT STREET
It's important to remember the bad things that people did in the past so that we don't make the same mistakes again.
HOLD FAST TO DREAMS FOR IF DREAMS DIE LIFE IS A BROKEN-WINGED BIRD THAT CANNOT FLY
Another clue. Off I go!
Another dark time in history

Iziko Slave Lodge Museum

This building looks nice today, but in the 1700's, it was a very sad place.

At this time, the Dutch East India Company captured many people from India, Southeast Asia, and East Africa and enslaved them. They brought them to South Africa. They sold some enslaved people to work in houses or on farms. Other enslaved people were forced to work for the Dutch East India Company. These enslaved people lived here in this building, which was known as the Slave Lodge.

Visiting historical places helps us understand history even better.

The inside of the Slave Lodge looks spacious now, but it was very different in the 1700's. There were no windows, so it was very dark. The basement often flooded and the roof leaked, so it was wet. Conditions were crowded, dirty, and very uncomfortable for the enslaved people.

Slavery was outlawed in South Africa in 1834. This building became government offices and then a cultural museum, known as the Iziko Slave Lodge Museum. Some of the items on display here include slave handcuffs and chains. They help us to understand the story of slavery in Cape Town.

Many Capetonians are descendants (children over many generations) of enslaved people from Africa, Asia, and India. South Africa has been called a "Rainbow Nation" because of its mix of peoples and cultures.

Bo-Kaap

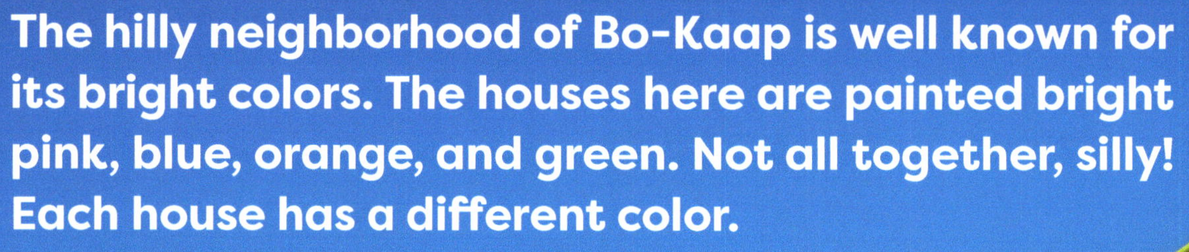

The hilly neighborhood of Bo-Kaap is well known for its bright colors. The houses here are painted bright pink, blue, orange, and green. Not all together, silly! Each house has a different color.

Bo-Kaap is one of Cape Town's oldest neighborhoods. In the late 1700's, Dutch colonists brought enslaved people from Southeast Asia to Cape Town. The Dutch had set up colonies in Southeast Asia in the 1600's. These people became known as the Cape Malay. Many of them settled in Bo-Kaap.

Originally, all of the houses in Bo-Kaap were white. They were rented out to the enslaved people, who weren't allowed to paint them. Once the enslaved people were free and allowed to buy the houses, it is said that they started painting their houses bright colors to celebrate their freedom.

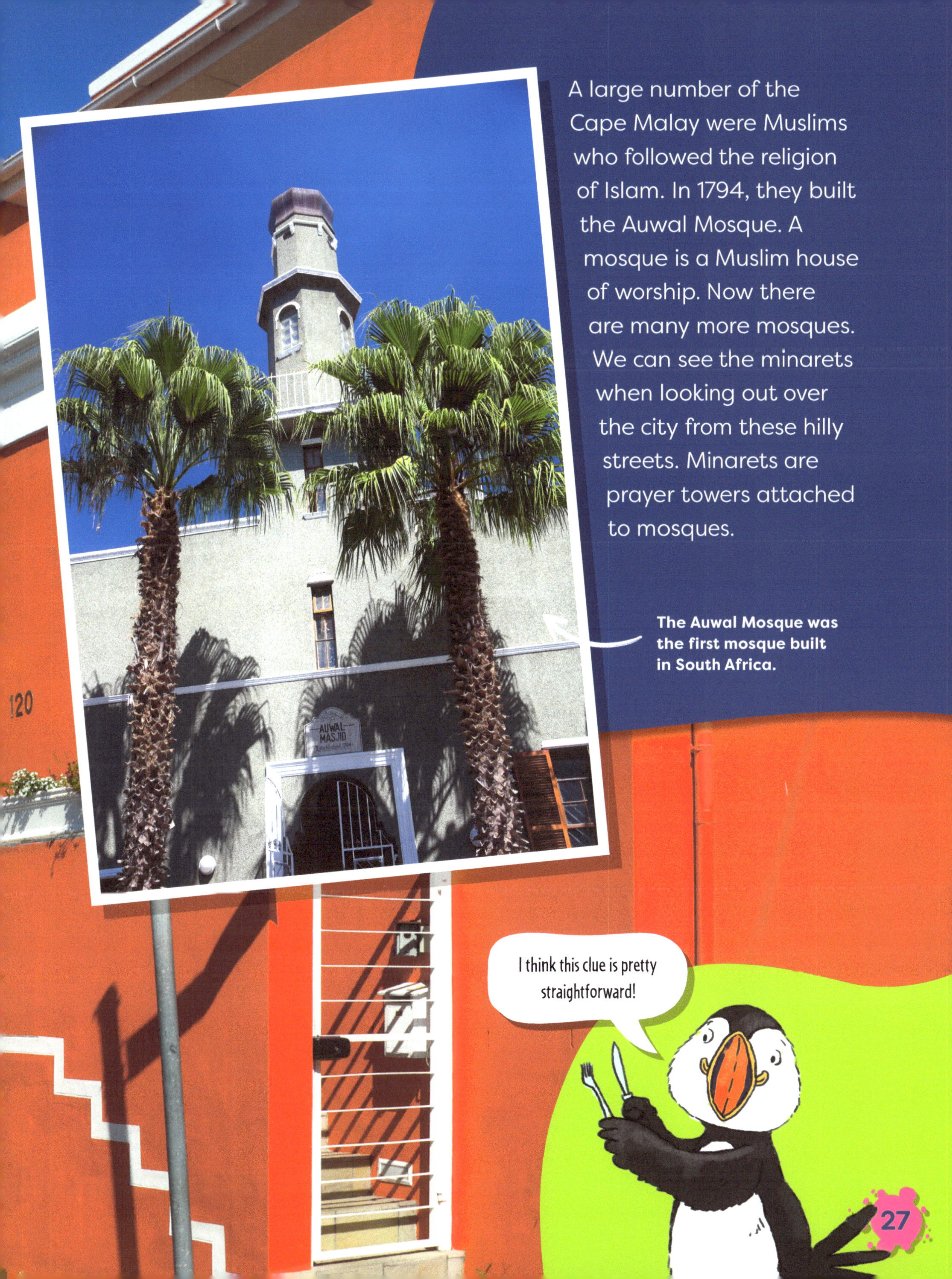

A large number of the Cape Malay were Muslims who followed the religion of Islam. In 1794, they built the Auwal Mosque. A mosque is a Muslim house of worship. Now there are many more mosques. We can see the minarets when looking out over the city from these hilly streets. Minarets are prayer towers attached to mosques.

The Auwal Mosque was the first mosque built in South Africa.

Let's eat!

It must be time to eat now! Good timing – I'm starving!

Capetonians enjoy many cultures and flavors. I'd like to try a little bit of everything. As we're in Bo-Kaap, let's look for bobotie.

The Cape Malay are known for this dish. It's baked in a deep pan, like a pie. But it's made with ground-up lamb or beef and curry spice, with egg custard on top. Curry is a popular flavor in Asia and India, where many of Cape Town's Coloured people have their roots. Have you ever tried bobotie before?

Bobotie is often served with rice cooked with spices and raisins. The spices give the rice a yellow color.

Mmmm, I smell a barbecue! In Cape Town, the word for barbecue is braai. Many Capetonians like to cook a spicy coil of sausage on the braai. It's called boerewors.

What goes with barbecued meat? One traditional African side dish is pap. That's a cornmeal porridge. What do you eat at a barbecue where you live?

This man is cooking boerewors on the braai. These sausages are made of beef mixed with lamb or pork, and are flavored with different spices.

Heart of Cape Town Museum

Don't be worried – we're in a museum ... not an operating theater!

The Heart of Cape Town Museum isn't far from a real-life operating theater. It's actually inside the Groote Schuur Hospital. What's so special about this hospital? The first successful human heart transplant surgery happened here. That means that someone got a heart from someone else!

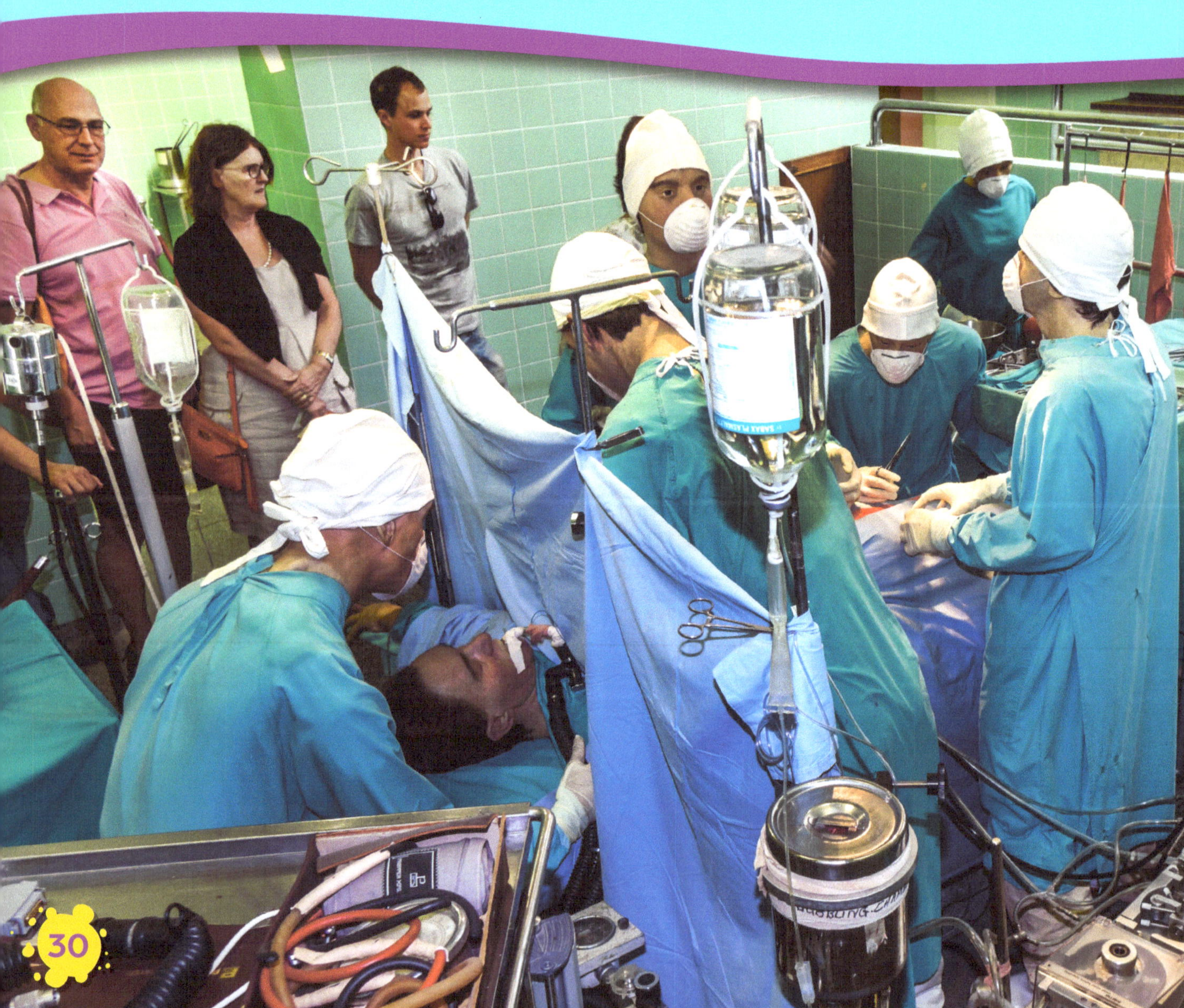

At the museum, you can take a tour of the operating room where the surgery happened! There's no blood, but there are all kinds of medical machines and instruments. Life-sized figures make the room look just like it did on the day of the surgery: December 3, 1967. On that day, Dr. Christiaan Barnard made history. He put a donated heart from the body of a dead person into the chest of patient Louis Washkansky. The heart began to beat strongly. The doctor said in Afrikaans, "Dit gaan werk!" That means, "It's going to work!"

Today, around 5,000 heart transplants take place every year across the world. This incredible operation has saved the lives of many people. And it all started right here!

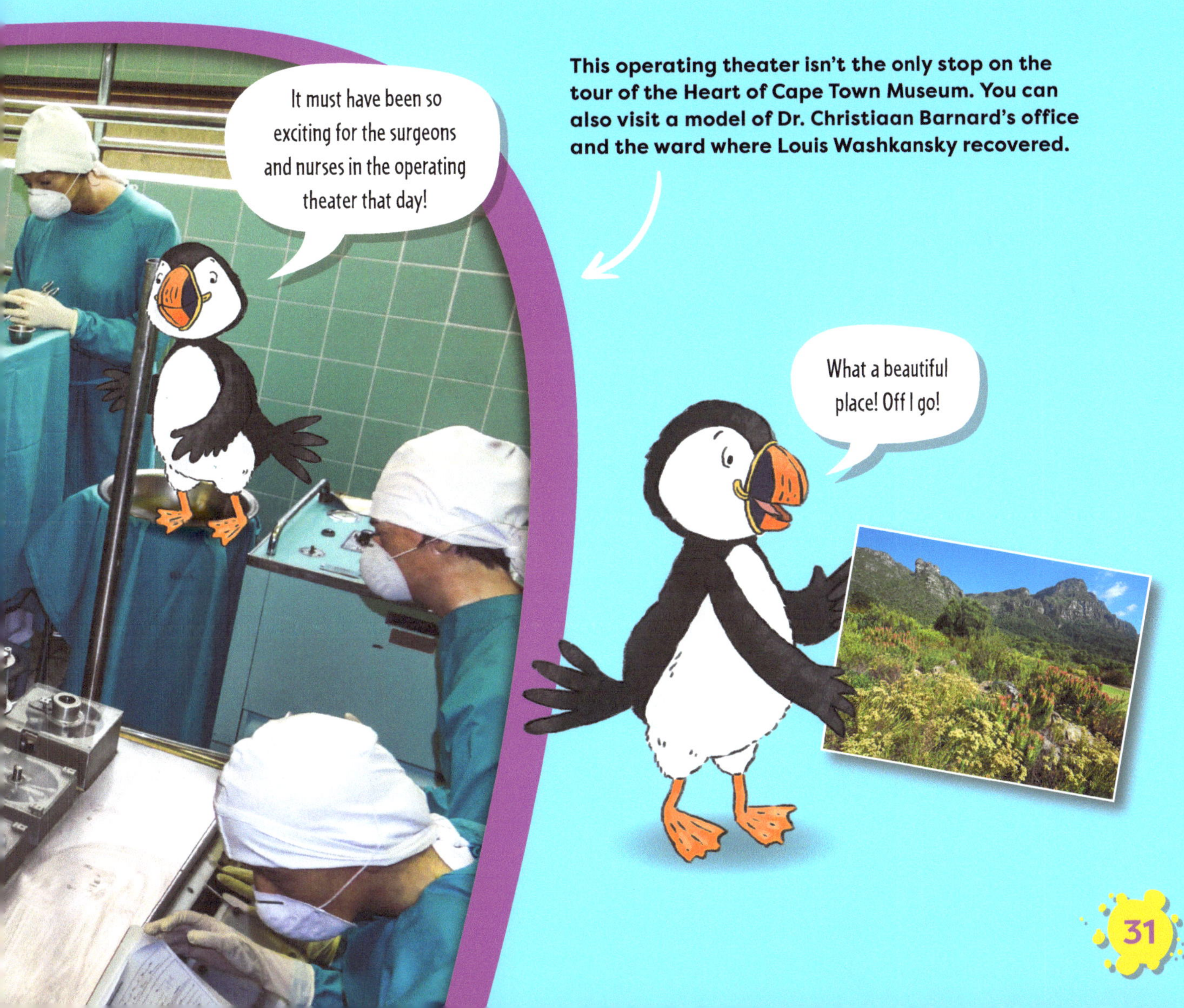

This operating theater isn't the only stop on the tour of the Heart of Cape Town Museum. You can also visit a model of Dr. Christiaan Barnard's office and the ward where Louis Washkansky recovered.

Kirstenbosch National Botanical Garden

Welcome to the Kirstenbosch National Botanical Garden.

This huge park is on the eastern slopes of Table Mountain and is home to a special kind of environment called fynbos. Fynbos comes from Dutch words meaning fine bush. Many kinds of small bushes and trees bloom in a burst of color in the South African spring, from August to November.

The gardens here are full of life. Cape Crag lizards sleep on sunny rocks. Tortoises creep through the plants and over mountain slopes. More than 125 different species of birds have been spotted, including sugarbirds, sunbirds, and a spotted eagle owl. If you are very lucky, you might catch a glimpse of a water mongoose or a Cape clawless otter in or around a stream.

The Tree Canopy Walkway winds through the treetops, giving incredible panoramic views of the park. People sometimes call it the boomslang, a kind of African tree snake, because the walkway is curvy like a snake. In some places, it dips down to touch the forest floor, before rising up to 36 feet (12 meters) above the ground.

Hout Bay

If you want to spot seals near Cape Town, Hout Bay is the place! The mountains drop right into the sea here.

The ocean water can be chilly on the cape's west side. Seals love to hang out in the harbor, where the boats dock. Did you know thousands of Cape fur seals live on Duiker Island just offshore? Some people call it Seal Island. You can take a boat tour to see them. Young seals, called pups, are born between late November and early December (that's spring in South Africa).

The Cape fur seal only lives on the coast of southern Africa.

I've got lots of souvenirs to bring back to my friends and family!

If you visit Hout Bay on the weekend, take a stroll through the Bay Harbour Market. This is a great place to buy souvenirs from local craftspeople. There's also live music from local bands.

If you want to relax, there's a beautiful white sand beach. And wait, I think I smell deep-fried fish and chips (French fries)? Mmmm! Lots of restaurants here have this tasty dish on their menu. The fish is caught on local fishing boats. Have you ever tried fish and chips before?

Muizenberg Beach

Muizenberg Beach is famous for its brightly colored shacks, called "bathing boxes." They're an old British tradition.

This beach near Cape Town is a fun place to swim, learn to surf, or just play in the sand. If we stick around long enough, we might see – and smell! – people barbecuing boerewors right on the beach.

Muizenberg Beach is found on False Bay, southeast of downtown Cape Town. False Bay got its name long ago from sailors. They were disappointed when they sailed into this bay thinking it was Table Bay. After their long journey from the East Indies, they were ready for the refreshment station!

Ocean currents bring warmer waters into False Bay, making it more pleasant to swim here. False Bay is home to many animals, including dolphins, whales, great white sharks, and orcas! If you're feeling brave, you can dive in an underwater cage to see the sharks up close.

This humpback whale in False Bay is breaching, or jumping out of the water with most of its body. Scientists believe that whales breach to communicate with each other.

A snoek? These clues are getting harder and harder!

Seek out a snoek

Kalk Bay

It turns out that a snoek (snook) is a type of fish that is often caught off the coast of South Africa. And what better place to try one than here in Kalk Bay?!

This town has a fishing harbor where people sell freshly caught fish right out of the boats! Snoek are eaten smoked, braaied (barbecued), dried, or salted. Which way sounds good to you?

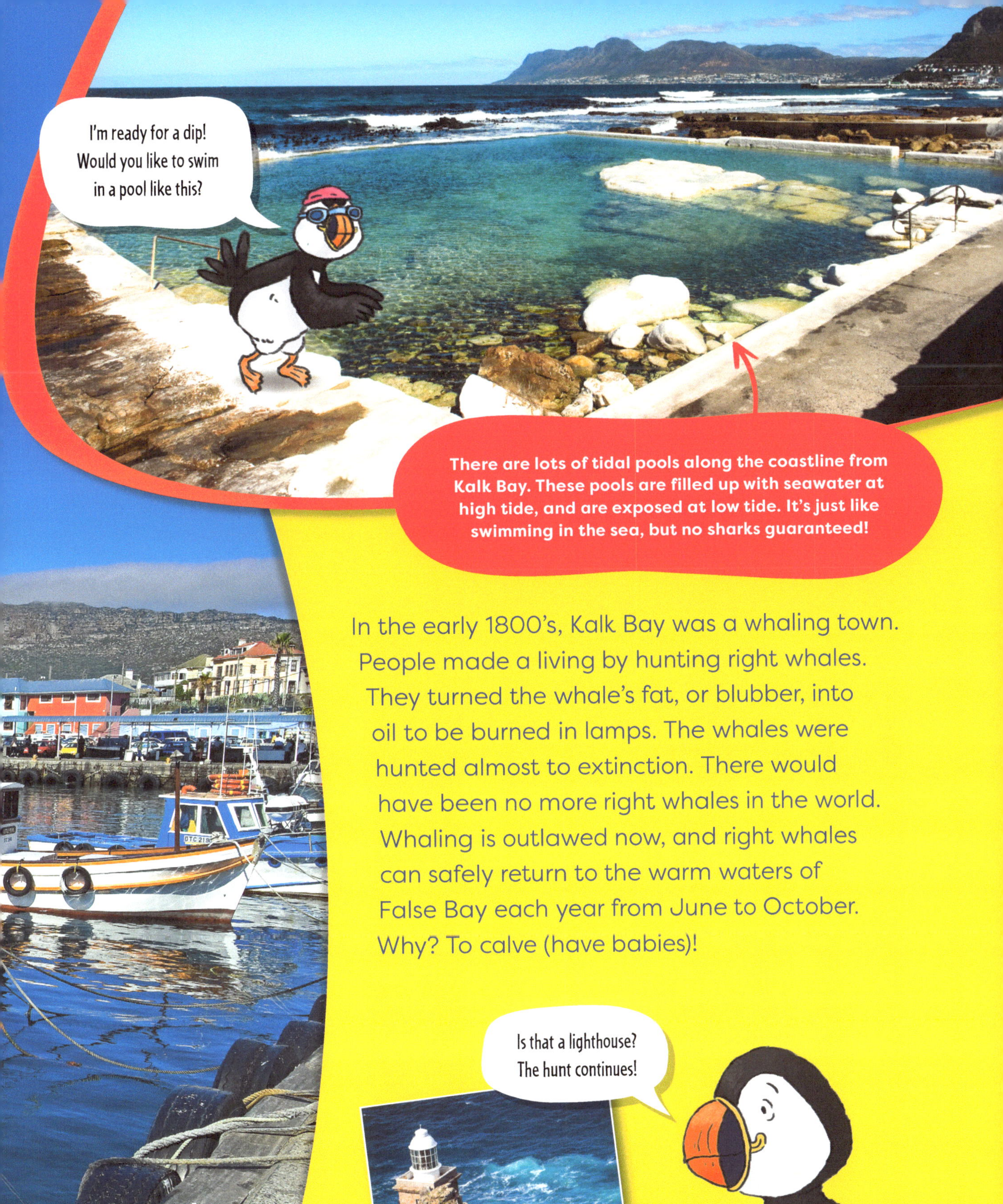

There are lots of tidal pools along the coastline from Kalk Bay. These pools are filled up with seawater at high tide, and are exposed at low tide. It's just like swimming in the sea, but no sharks guaranteed!

In the early 1800's, Kalk Bay was a whaling town. People made a living by hunting right whales. They turned the whale's fat, or blubber, into oil to be burned in lamps. The whales were hunted almost to extinction. There would have been no more right whales in the world. Whaling is outlawed now, and right whales can safely return to the warm waters of False Bay each year from June to October. Why? To calve (have babies)!

Can you spot the lighthouse down below on Cape Point? This is the southern tip of the Cape Peninsula (also known as the Cape of Good Hope).

The Cape of Good Hope was once called the Cape of Storms. Bad weather made it hard for sailors to steer their ships around the cape. Lots of rocks hide below the water's surface, too. See the waves breaking on them? At least 26 ships have wrecked here. On the Shipwreck Trail, you can see one that ran aground and is still on the beach. The lighthouse helps to prevent any more shipwrecks. It is the most powerful lighthouse on the coast of South Africa! Every 30 seconds, it flashes three times.

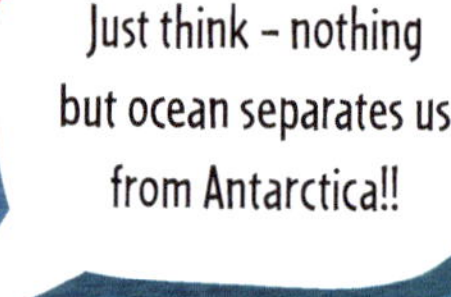

lighthouse

It's a long way up to the top of Cape Point, so I'm going to ride the funicular railway. A funicular railway has two cars connected by a cable. As one car goes downhill, it helps to pull the other one up.

The funicular railway is named the Flying Dutchman, after a legendary ghost ship. Long ago, an entire ship is said to have disappeared while sailing around the cape. Legend says the ghostly ship and her crew still haunt these waters.

Boulders Beach

Black and white ... penguins?!? In South Africa?

That's right! Penguins don't just live in freezing Antarctica. Some species live on the coasts of Africa, South America, and Australia. The penguins that live here on Boulders Beach are African penguins. Nearly 2,500 African penguins live around the beach's giant granite boulders. That may sound like a lot, but this species of penguin is actually endangered. That means

they are in danger of going extinct. (You know what that means – there wouldn't be any more of them.) They are affected by pollution, people catching too many fish, and habitat destruction. So even though they are cute, you shouldn't get too close. And in any case, they bite!

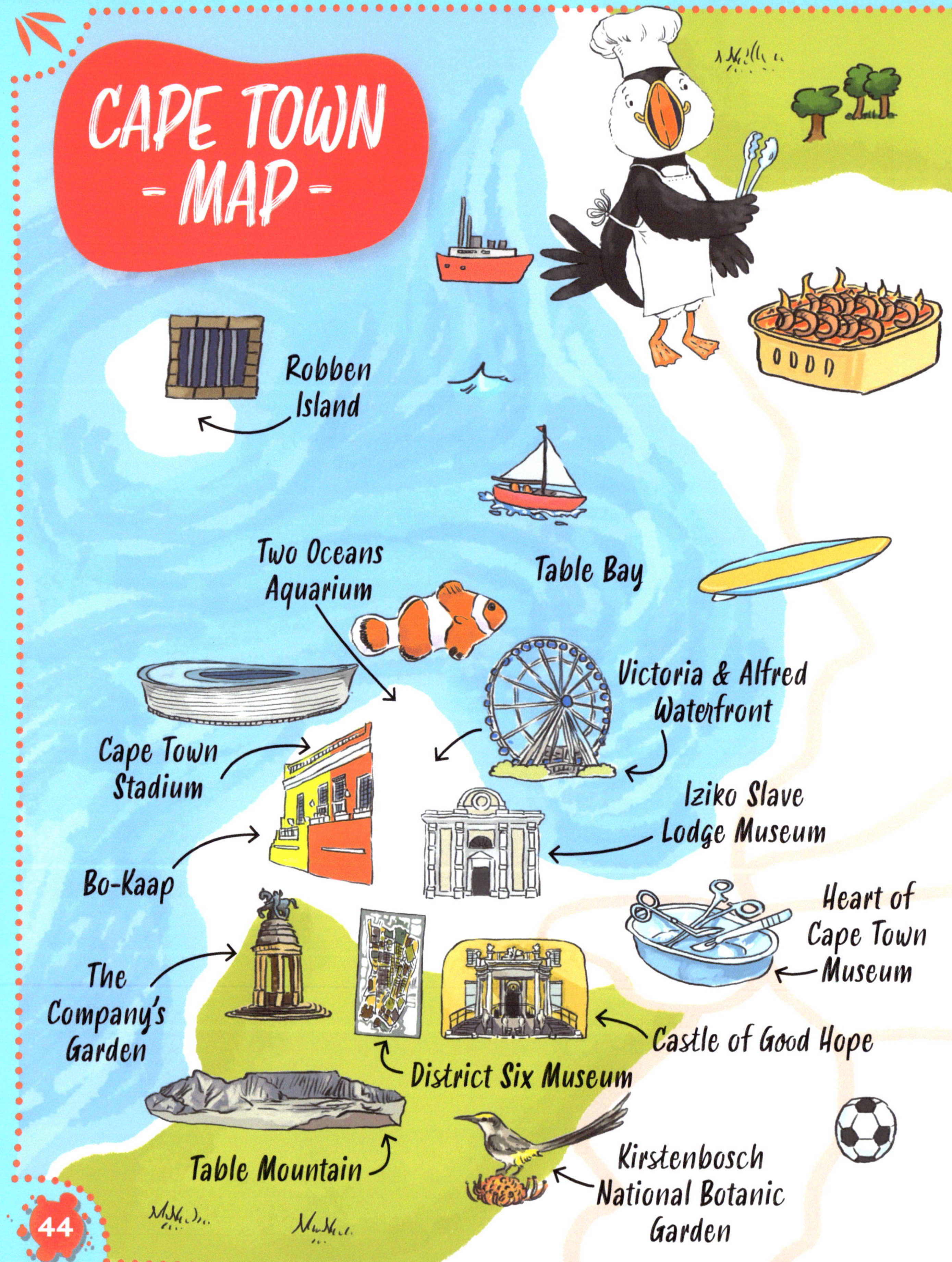
CAPE TOWN
- MAP -
Robben Island
Table Bay
Two Oceans Aquarium
Victoria & Alfred Waterfront
Cape Town Stadium
Iziko Slave Lodge Museum
Bo-Kaap
Heart of Cape Town Museum
The Company's Garden
Castle of Good Hope
District Six Museum
Table Mountain
Kirstenbosch National Botanic Garden

Central Cape Town
(see large map)
Hout Bay
Muizenberg
Beach
Kalk Bay
Boulders
Beach
Cape Point

A Day in Cape Town

What a beautiful morning! Fill up on mealie pap, a breakfast porridge enjoyed with sugar and milk or golden syrup and butter.

Let's hope you had a large breakfast because you're going to need the fuel! It's time for hiking at Lion's Head Trail.

This climb may be a challenge, but the panoramic views of the city and the coastline are well worth it.

All that climbing probably worked up your appetite! Make your way to the Victoria & Alfred Waterfront for some lunch. Don't forget to take a ride on the Ferris wheel!

This museum will teach you the history of slavery in Cape Town and South Africa.

It is important to learn the history of the places we visit, so travel to the Iziko Slave Lodge Museum. Remembering the bad things people did in the past can help us avoid those mistakes in the future.

Round out your day with some shopping on Long Street in the City Bowl neighborhood. It's home to wonderful antique shops as well as many bookstores. What gifts or souvenirs will you pick up?

End your busy day in Cape Town with some dinner at one of the many great African or Indian restaurants in the brightly colored Bo-Kaap neighborhood.

Treat yourself to some sweet malva pudding made with apricot jam before you turn in for the night.

Where Am I?

Destination 1

Completed in 1679, this is the oldest colonial building in all South Africa.

This yellow building was designed in the shape of a five-pointed star so soldiers could defend attacks from any direction.

In the past, this building included apartments, a church, a bakery, offices, and jail cells, but today it is a national monument and has many museums.

Destination 2

Today, this destination is a museum. It is also home to a nature reserve where visitors can see tortoises, antelope, and fur seals.

This location was a famous South African prison where inmates had to work in quarries, and their cells were small and basic.

Nelson Mandela spent 18 of his 27 years in jail here for working against the government and apartheid.

Destination 3

Tidal pools line the coast of this destination, naturally filling with salt water at high tide and emptying out at low tide.

This is the perfect destination to try freshly caught snoek, whether it is smoked, braaied, dried, or salted!

Every June to October, whales return to these warm waters to calve.

Destination 4

This destination was designed to look like the traditional hats worn by the Venda women of northern South Africa.

Football, rugby, cricket, tennis, concerts, and other events frequently draw large, loud crowds to this location.

This stadium was originally built to host the 2010 World Cup, a famous international football (American soccer) tournament held once every four years.

Destination 5

You may find cute little animals called rock hyrax here. They may look like hamsters but are actually related to elephants!

It's 900 feet (3,000 meters) to the top of this destination so get ready for a big hike or save your energy and ride the cable car.

This destination is known for its iconic, flat top.

Destination 6

This destination can be found right inside Groote Schuur Hospital!

Today, you can tour the operating room to learn about medical machines and instruments that keep us healthy.

The first successful human heart transplant took place here on December 3, 1967.

Photos from Cape Town

District 6 Museum

Table Mountain

Boulders Beach

Muizenberg Beach

Cape Point

Kirstenbosch National Botanical Garden

Bo-Kaap

Engage Your Reader

Activate background knowledge, set the purpose for reading, and monitor comprehension with this tried-and-true reading strategy!

Work with your reader(s) to create a KWL chart. Take some time to discuss what students already KNOW about Cape Town as well as what they WONDER about the city. You will revisit what they LEARNED after reading the book.

KNOW	WONDER	LEARNED

1. Have readers preview the structure of this text by flipping through the pages. Page 5 describes how clues are included for Norrie the puffin's next destinations.
2. Set the tone for reading: *As you read, think about all the different places in Cape Town and how history, culture, and people have shaped them into what they are today.*
3. After reading each section, revisit the KWL chart. Brainstorm what readers LEARNED from this section and add it to the chart. Your reader can add other wonderings they may have had, too!

Consider these questions to guide the brainstorming process:

- Why is location important to places, history, and culture?
- What patterns do you notice in the placement of things around the city of Cape Town?
- What makes Cape Town unique?

Use these comprehension questions to help your reader(s) check their understanding as they navigate the text.

p. 6-7 How did Table Mountain get its name?
What are peninsulas and capes?

p. 8-9 What did Captain Jan van Riebeeck begin at Table Bay in 1652? How might that have affected how this bay is used today?

p. 10-11 What would you enjoy doing most at Victoria & Alfred Waterfront?

p. 12-13 Describe what types of marine life you can see and learn about at Two Oceans Aquarium.

p. 14-15 Why is Robben Island historically significant?
Who was Nelson Mandela?

p. 16-17 What makes South Africa's national anthem unique?
For what is Cape Town Stadium used?

p. 18-19 How was the Castle of Good Hope used in the past?

p. 20-21 How has The Company's Garden been used over time?

p. 22-23 Why is it important to have museums like this dedicated to bad times in history?

p. 24-25 Why was the Iziko Slave Lodge originally built, and how is the building used today?

p. 26-27 According to the text, how were the houses in the Bo-Kaap neighborhood said to get their bright colors?

p. 28-29 Of the Capetonian food described, what would you most like to try? Why?

p. 30-31 What medical marvel took place on December 3, 1967?

p. 32-33 What wildlife might you see when visiting Kirstenbosch National Botanical Garden?
Why is the Tree Canopy Walkway sometimes called a boomslang?

p. 34-35 What is Seal Island?

p. 36-37 How did False Bay get its name?
Why might Muizenberg Beach be a popular location for people to swim and surf?

p. 38-39 Explain what has happened to the whales of Kalk Bay over time.

p. 40-41 By what other names is Cape Point known and how did it get its nickname?
Why is the lighthouse on Cape Point so important?

p. 42-43 Why should we be concerned about the African penguins of Boulders Beach?

Extend Through Writing

Norrie the puffin just took you on a tour of Cape Town, South Africa! Based on the places highlighted in this book, where would you like to visit in Cape Town?

Your written response should include:

- An introduction, including a general statement about Cape Town
- At least three places you would like to visit and at least three reasons why these places interest you
- A conclusion in which you briefly restate your interest in these three famous Cape Town destinations

Copy this graphic organizer onto another sheet of paper or visit **www.worldbook.com/resources** to download and print a copy. Use it to help you plan your writing.

Introduction:		
Destination 1	Destination 2	Destination 3
Reason 1	Reason 1	Reason 1
Reason 2	Reason 2	Reason 2
Reason 3	Reason 3	Reason 3
Conclusion:		

Answers

Where Am I? answers, p. 48-49:

1. Castle of Good Hope, 2. Robben Island, 3. Kalk Bay, 4. Cape Town Stadium, 5. Table Mountain, 6. Heart of Cape Town Museum

Comprehension question answers, p. 53:

p. 6-7

Table Mountain got its name because the top of the mountain is flat, just like a table.

A peninsula is an area of land almost completely surrounded by water. A cape is a piece of land that sticks out into the ocean.

p. 8-9

In 1652, Captain Jan van Riebeeck first sailed into Table Bay. Because he and his crew were going to make many trips here, he began to build a refreshment station. This eventually became a major European settlement, and today the area houses a major port.

p. 10-11

Answers may vary.

p. 12-13

Two Oceans Aquarium visitors can learn about many types of marine life around South Africa, including over 100 species of shark. They can also see a massive kelp forest and step into a glass dome to see what it is like under the water.

p. 14-15

Today, Robben Island is a museum, but in the past it was a very harsh prison that held many nonwhite people during apartheid.

Nelson Mandela spent 27 years in prison (18 of them here) because he worked against the government and apartheid. After being freed, he was elected President of South Africa in 1994, during the first election in which nonwhite people were allowed to vote.

p. 16-17

South Africa's national anthem is unique because it includes five languages: Xhosa, Zulu, Sesotho, Afrikaans, and English.

Cape Town Stadium has hosted the World Cup football tournament as well as other sporting events like rugby, cricket, and tennis. It is a popular location for concerts, too.

p. 18-19

In the past, the Castle of Good Hope was used to defend against invaders. It was so big, it included apartments, a church, a bakery, offices, and even jails.

p. 20-21

The Company's Garden was originally a vegetable garden for the Dutch East India Company's sailors. Today, it is home to large trees and plants, an herb garden, and a rose garden for visitors to enjoy.

p. 22-23

It is important for museums to share about bad things that have happened throughout history so we as a society can learn from our mistakes.

p. 24-25

The Iziko Slave Lodge was originally built to house enslaved people who were forced to work in homes and on farms. Today, it has been converted into a national monument with museums so people can understand the story of slavery in Cape Town and South Africa.

p. 26-27

According to the text, it is said that previously owned slaves celebrated their freedom by painting the houses in Bo-Kaap bright colors.

p. 28-29

Answers may vary.

p. 30-31

On December 3, 1967, Dr. Christiaan Barnard made history by completing the first successful human heart transplant surgery.

p. 32-33

You can expect to see bushes, trees, lizards, tortoises, and over 125 different species of birds when visiting Kirstenbosch National Botanical Garden.

The Tree Canopy Walkway is sometimes called a boomslang because it looks like a slithering tree snake common to Africa by the same name.

p. 34-35

Seal Island is a nickname for Duiker Island just offshore of Cape Town. You can even take a tour and meet the seals that call this island home!

p. 36-37

Many years ago, sailors hoping to find Cape Bay accidentally sailed into False Bay and, disappointed, named it accordingly.

Muizenberg Beach may be a popular place to swim and surf due to the warm ocean currents and the iconic bathing boxes.

p. 38-39

In the early 1800's, many people practiced whaling to gather blubber for lamp oil. This hunting almost caused whales to go extinct! Since then, laws have been passed to help prevent whaling. Now, whales return to False Bay each year to calve.

p. 40-41

Cape Point is also known as the Cape of Good Hope and the Cape of Storms. It got its latter nickname because of the bad weather that makes sailing around the cape quite dangerous.

The lighthouse on Cape Point is important because it helps prevent shipwrecks.

p. 42-43

People should be concerned about the African penguins of Boulders Beach because they are an endangered species. They may go extinct because of pollution, overfishing, and habitat destruction caused by humans.

Glossary

Afrikaans *(af ruh KAHNS)* A language made by many groups of people who lived or settled in South Africa. Those groups include Dutch, French, and German settlers, native people, and enslaved people from Asia and Africa.

apartheid *(ah PAHRT hayt)* A set of South African laws that kept people of different races separate. It sorted people into different groups – Black, white, Coloured (mixed race), and Asian. These groups were separated in all areas of life, including school, homes, jobs, and transportation.

boerewors *(BOO rih vohrs)* Spicy sausage shaped into a coil

Capetonian *(kayp TOH nee uhn)* A person who lives in Cape Town

cobblestone *(KOB uhl stohn)* Rounded bricks used for making streets

colony, colonial *(KOL uh nee, kuh LOH nee uhl)* A colony is a settlement started by people outside their native land. It is ruled by their home country.

enslaved *(ehn SLAYVD)* **person** A person who is owned by another person. Enslaved people work without pay. Enslaved people are often brought against their will from one place or country to another.

peninsula *(puh NIHN suh luh)* An area of land that is nearly surrounded by water. Peninsulas are usually long, narrow strips of land.

township *(TOWN shihp)* In South Africa, an area on the edge of the city set aside for Black people to live in under apartheid. Townships were known for their poor housing, and lack of electricity and running water.

Index

www.ingramcontent.com/pod-product-compliance
Ingram Content Group UK Ltd.
Pitfield, Milton Keynes, MK11 3LW, UK
UKHW060104300726
14090UKWH00003B/375

9780716653264